The Waterman/Harewood Piano Ser...

Young Pianist's Repertoire Book 1

Selected classics old and new

Faber Music Limited

London

Contents

Grateful acknowledgements are made to the following for permission to reprint copyright material: Boosey & Hawkes (London) for 'March' and 'Valse' from *Six Children's Pieces* by Shostakovich; Editions Billaudot (Paris) for 'Waltz of Beauty and the Prince' by Paule Maurice; Mills Music Ltd (London) for 'Friday' from *Seven Days A Week* by Richard Rodney Bennett; Schott & Co. Ltd (London) for 'Jazz-Etudiette', from *Easy Dances* by Mátyás Seiber; Universal Edition (London) Ltd for 'Negro Spiritual' from *Double Dozen for Small Fingers* by Jenö Takács and 'Pony Ride' from *Playground* by Anthony Hedges; Panton (Prague) for 'Five Czech Folk Songs' by Petr Eben.

This collection ©1969 by Faber Music Ltd
First published in 1969 by Faber Music Ltd
This edition ©1983 by Faber Music Ltd
This edition published in 1983 by Faber Music Ltd
3 Queen Square London WC1N 3AU
Music drawn by Christopher Hinkins
Cover design by Shirley Tucker
Photograph by Ben Johnson
Printed in England by Halstan & Co. Ltd

King William's March

JEREMIAH CLARKE
(1659-1707)

Alla Marcia

f con brio

mf

f

Prelude

HENRY PURCELL
(1659-1695)

Menuet en Rondeau

JEAN PHILIPPE RAMEAU
(1683-1764)

Gavotte and Gigue

SAMUEL ARNOLD
(1740-1802)

Gavotte

Grazioso

Gigue

Allegro con brio

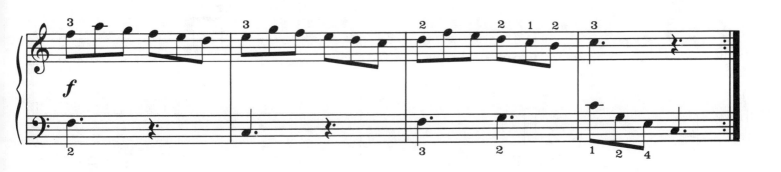

Allegro

SAMUEL ARNOLD

Entrée

(from the Wolfgang Notebook, 1762)*

Collected by LEOPOLD MOZART

(1719-1787)

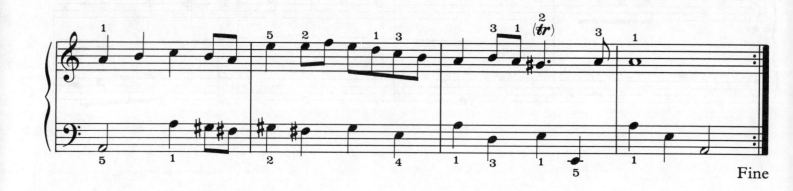

Fine

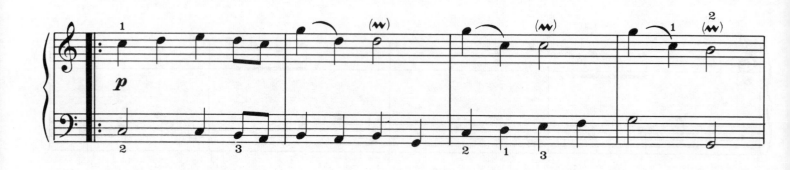

Da Capo al Fine

*Leopold Mozart compiled a collection of pieces of music of the time and gave them to his son Wolfgang on his name-day on October 31st, 1762. Wolfgang was then six years old, and he played these pieces at informal concerts at home. Nannerl Mozart, Wolfgang's elder sister by five years, also had a book of pieces collected for her by her father.

Nannerl's Minuet

(from the Nannerl Notebook, 1759)

Collected by LEOPOLD MOZART

Burlesque

(Old folk-tune from the Wolfgang Notebook)

Collected by LEOPOLD MOZART

Angloise

(from the Wolfgang Notebook)

Collected by LEOPOLD MOZART

Musette
(from the Wolfgang Notebook)

Collected by LEOPOLD MOZART

(sempre stacc.)

Minuet in G

JOHANN SEBASTIAN BACH
(1685-1750)

Minuet in G minor

(from the Anna Magdalena Notebook of 1725)
BWV Anh.115

JOHANN SEBASTIAN BACH

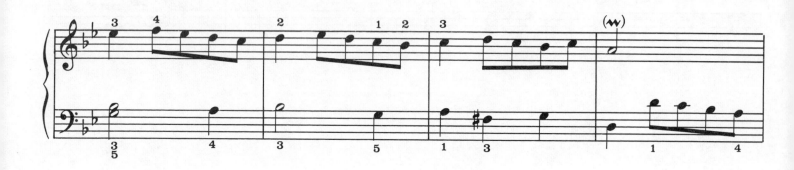

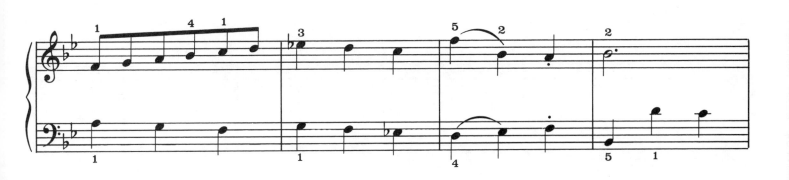

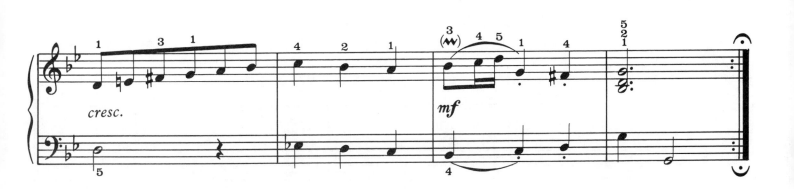

Duet for Two Hands

'Impertinence'

GEORGE FRIDERIC HANDEL

(1685-1759)

Bourrée

GEORGE FRIDERIC HANDEL

Sonatina

TOBIAS HASLINGER
(1787-1842)

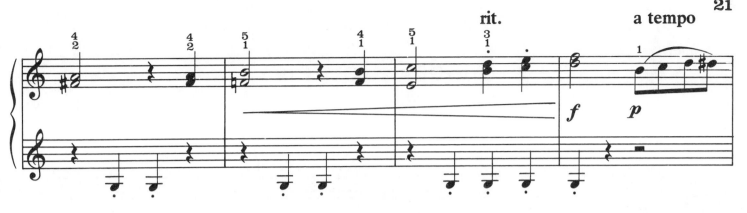

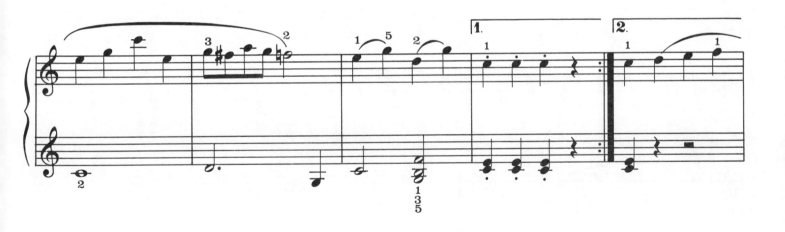

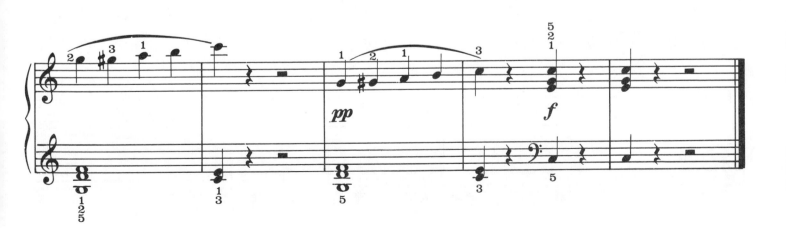

Sunday Morning

CARL CZERNY
(1791-1857)

Alexander March

CARL CZERNY

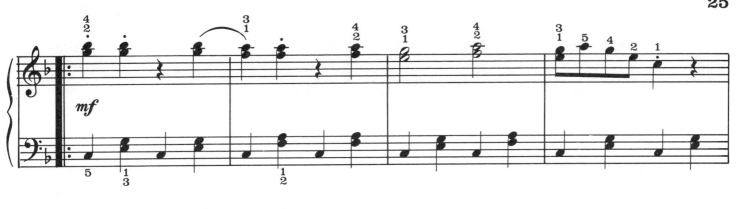

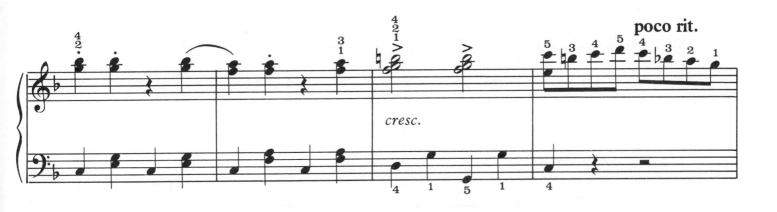

German Song

CARL CZERNY

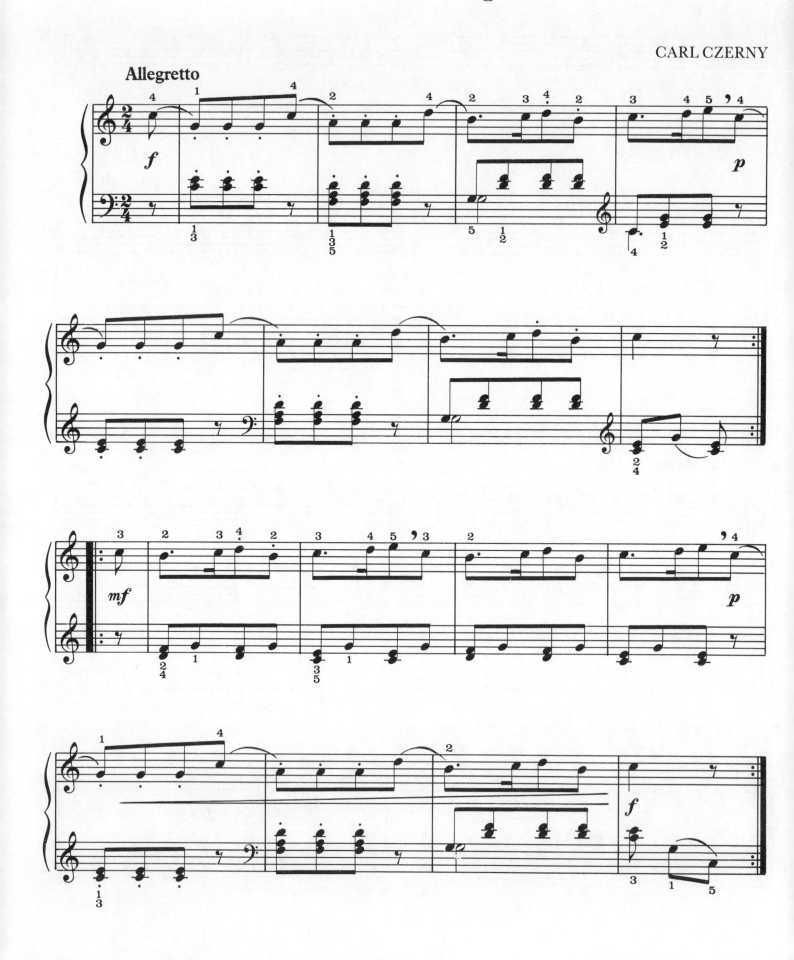

Ecossaise

LUDWIG VAN BEETHOVEN
(1770-1827)

Old French Song

Op.39 no.16

PETER ILYICH TCHAIKOWSKY

(1840-1893)

Melody

(from Album for the Young)
Op.68 no.1

ROBERT SCHUMANN
(1810-1856)

The fingerings in italics are Schumann's own.

Waltz of Beauty and the Prince

(from Once upon a Time)

PAULE MAURICE

Study

ALBERT LOESCHHORN
(1819-1905)

Allegro con brio

Pony Ride

(from Playground)

ANTHONY HEDGES

Negro Spiritual

(from Double Dozen for Small Fingers)

JENÖ TAKÁCS
(born 1902)

Hold sustaining pedal
down until end of piece

Friday
(from Seven Days a Week)

RICHARD RODNEY BENNETT
(born 1936)

Jazz – Etudiette

(from Easy Dances, II)

MÁTYÁS SEIBER
(1905-1960)

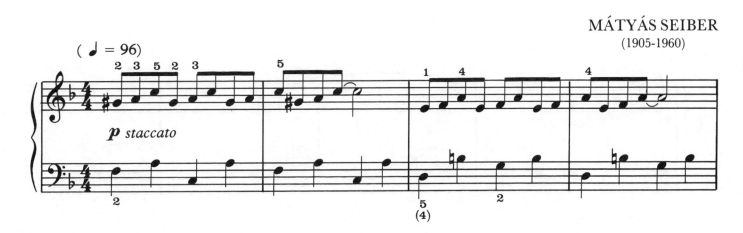

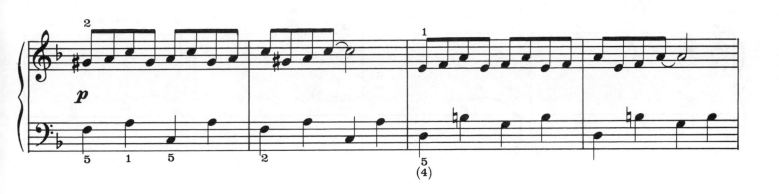

Waltz

(from Six Children's Pieces)

DIMITRI SHOSTAKOVITCH
(1906-1975)

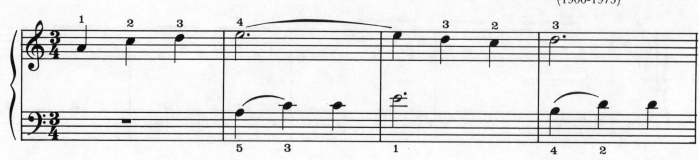

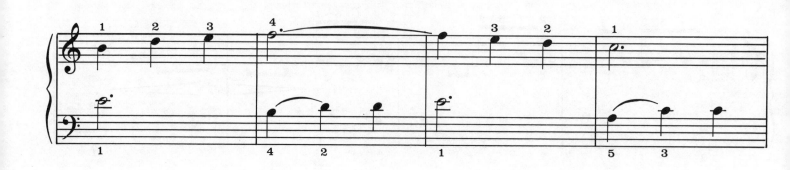

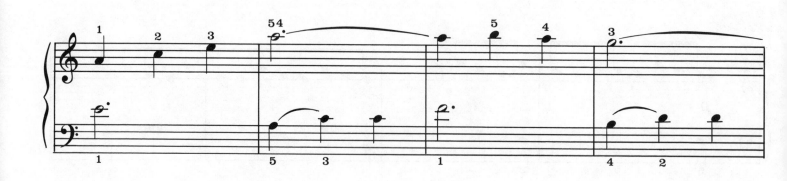

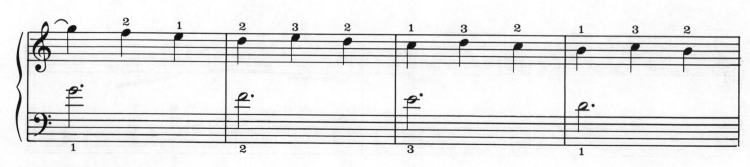

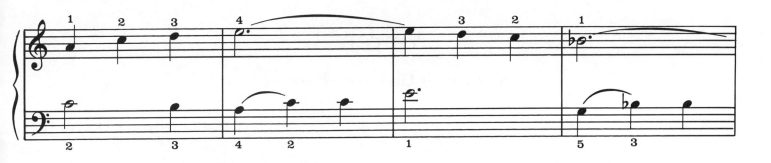

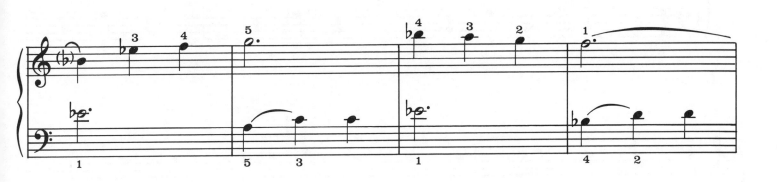

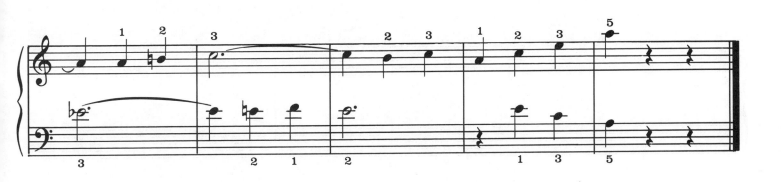

March

(from Six Children's Pieces)

DIMITRI SHOSTAKOVITCH

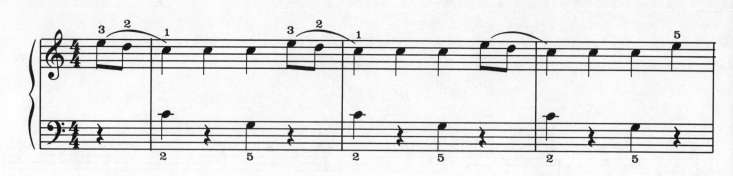

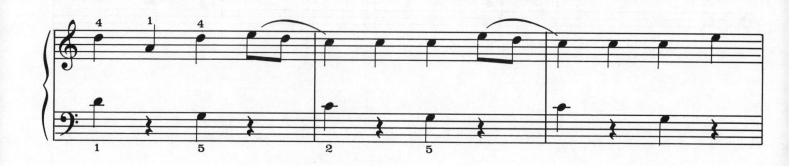

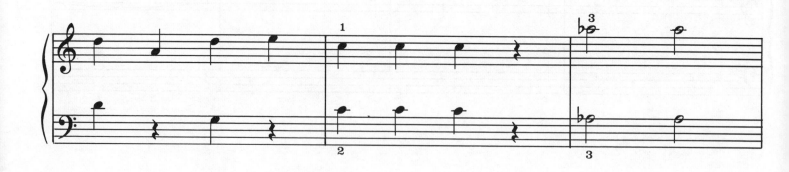

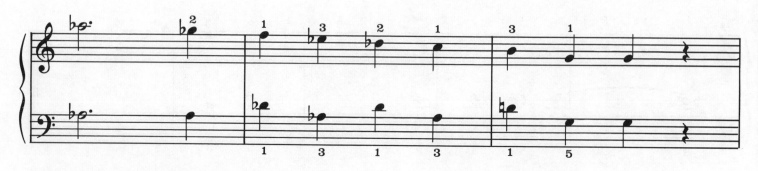

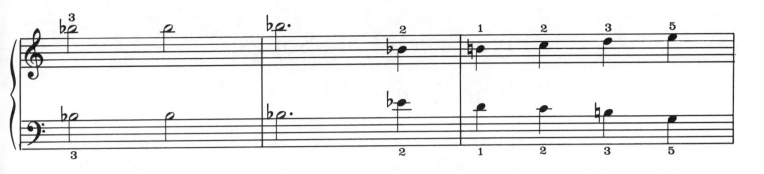

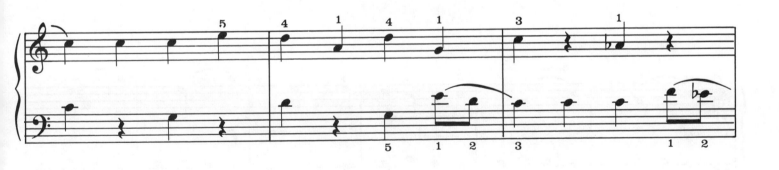

Five Czech Folk Songs:
The Rejected Lover

Arranged by PETR EBEN
(born 1929)

Our Old Stove is Bust Again

Arranged by PETR EBEN

Roses at the Cottage Window

Arranged by PETR EBEN

O, the Scent of Roses!

Arranged by PETR EBEN

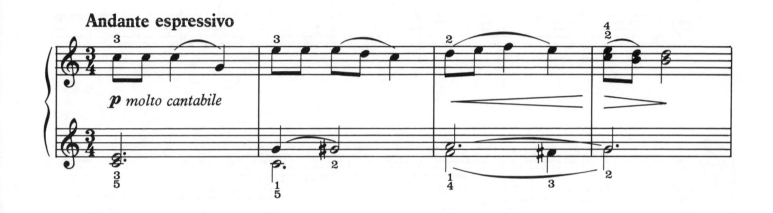

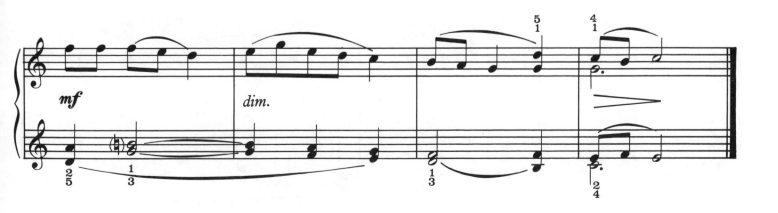

Too Bad for You, I Love Another

Arranged by PETR EBEN